ROCK
POINT

A division of the Quarto Publishing Group USA Inc.
276 Fifth Avenue Suite 206
New York, New York 10001

ROCK POINT and the distinctive Rock Point logo are
trademarks of the Quarto Publishing Group USA Inc.

This 2014 edition published by Rock Point
by arrangement with Harriet Ziefert, Inc.

ISBN-13: 978-1-6310-6013-7

Printed in China

2 4 6 8 10 9 7 5 3 1

www.rockpointpub.com

Little Miseries
LONDON

SPRING

SUMMER

FALL

WINTER

Illustrations by Peter Jarvis

Little
Miseries
LONDON

WINTER

THE QUEEN'S GUARD

Misery
is when the entire country
closes for two weeks for
the Christmas holidays.

Misery
is no public transport
anywhere in England on
Christmas day.

Misery
is no 24-hour Tube service.

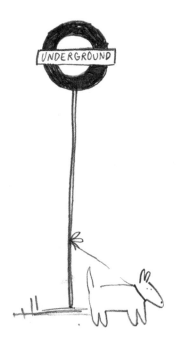

Misery is when one snowflake grinds public transportation to a complete halt.

Misery is the Tube that's freezing in winter...and as hot as a sauna in summer.

Misery is gritting the roads AFTER the frost.

Misery is a heating system at your workplace that bears no relationship to the weather outside.

LONDON EYE

Misery

is queues,

orderly or otherwise.

Misery
is the glass recycle
truck that arrives
at 5 A.M.

Misery
is the endless recycling
of junk mail.

Misery is hosting the entire family for Christmas lunch... and you only have a small table and four chairs.

Misery is finding ways to use leftover sprouts after Christmas.

Misery

is a Christmas
turkey that's too big
to fit in the oven.

Misery is fighting for a spot in Trafalgar Square on New Year's Eve.

Misery
is passengers
who stand
on the
walking half
of the
escalator.

Misery is a city with as many betting shops as banks.

Misery is paying your utilities bill.

bodorka / Shutterstock.com

Misery

is living under
the Heathrow flight path
and being awakened
by the early arrivals
at 4 A.M.

Misery
is when your Oyster card beeps,
but you cannot open the barrier.

Misery
is running for the bus,
tapping on the door,
smiling sweetly...
and the bus driver won't
oblige and open the door.

Misery is finding it impossible to get warm.

SPRING

Misery
is carrying your umbrella
everywhere, everyday.

Misery
is not being able to find an
empty spot on a park bench
on the first warm day.

BUCKINGHAM
PALACE

Misery

is expecting to find
a Boris bike and
none are available.

Misery
is The Tate Modern
between 7 and 9
on a Friday night.

Misery
is a trip to the
Museum of Natural History
to see the dinosaurs...
and meeting up with half
of London's families
with small children.

Misery is watching pedestrians overtake you while you're stuck in a taxi with the meter running.

Misery
is a taxi that takes only cash, instead of your credit card.

Misery
is living in a place called Cockfosters

Misery
is the parking warden
who does not see your
"Pay and Display" ticket.

Misery
is driving on
the M4 on
Friday afternoon.

Misery
is finding
the right exit
off the roundabout

Misery

is not being able to
go for a morning run
because dust from
the Sahara has descended.

Misery
is the paper that
flies around
on recycling day.

Misery
is blowing your nose
and seeing black snot
on the tissue.

Misery

is having yet another set
of visitors who ask to
be escorted to the Eye.

Misery

is rubbish all over
the front garden because
a fox has raided the bins.

Misery

is being asked
on the "way in"
and the "way out"
of the supermarket
if you want the Big Issue.

Misery

is people who use
one seat for their toddler,
and another for their
push chair and changing bag...
leaving no room for you.

THE GHERKIN

Misery

is the temporary deafness
of the bus driver
who does not stop,
even though you have pushed
the button more than once.

Misery

is seeing yourself
on the bus'
security camera.

Misery

is the arrival of "Bold and Naked Yoga" from New York and being asked by a friend to attend a Sunday class. Downward dog while naked? Forget it!

Misery

is when your haircutter moves to New York.

Misery
is interrupting your yoga class with a belch.

Misery
is being atop
an open bus
when it
starts to rain.

Little Miseries
LONDON

SUMMER

Misery

is being asked by an American for directions to Chis-WICK, LEI-chester Square, or Wimble-TON.

Misery
is the chilblains
after Ascot...

Misery
is buying strawberries
at Wimbledon
(£1 per berry!)

Misery

is waiting for officials
to decide whether
to call off, or just delay,
a cricket game
because of rain.

TOWER
BRIDGE

Misery is little blue bags of poo
left near the curb.

Misery
is tourists
who forget
this is a
functioning city,
not an
amusement park.

Misery
is trying to show
an out-of-town guest
the Rosetta Stone
along with 100
Italian teenagers.

Misery
is not being able
to understand
the announcements
on the Tube.

Misery
is being stuck under
a sweaty armpit
at rush hour.

Mornington Crescent
ss Cottage
St. John's Wood
Great Portland Street
Euston
Baker Street
Euston Square
Euston 200m
Warren Street
Regent's Park
Goodge Street
Holborn
Oxford Circus
Bond Street
Tottenham Court Road
Green Park
Leicester Square
Piccadilly Circus
Charing Cross
St. James's Park
Sloane Square
Westminster
Victoria

MIND

Misery is being caught behind the person who can't find his Oyster card at the barrier.

Misery
is pulling the emergency HELP cord instead of the light switch.

Misery is discovering a locust in your lunchtime salad.

Misery
is satellite nav that doesn't know about one-way streets

THE SHARD

Misery
is not finding
a rubbish bin
anywhere because
they've been
removed due to
security threats.

Misery is slinking into a restaurant to use the loo and trying to avoid contact with the staff...or pretending to be a customer and hoping you won't be caught.

Misery is having to make a reservation at The Ritz for high tea three months in advance.

Misery

is a busker in Covent Garden who can't sing on key.

THANKYOU

Misery is waking up in the middle of the night thinking your neighbor is dying, when in reality a fox is screaming outside.

Misery

is paying the
princely sum of
£15 to drive into
central London,
only to find all of
the parking spots
occupied.

Misery
is trying to not run over
the tourists that forget
to `look to the right!´

Misery is the price of petrol, public transportation, taxis, and car parks.

Misery
is hosepipe bans regardless of constant downpours.

Misery
is getting stuck
in the middle of a group
of tourists who are
following an umbrella.

Misery
is golf umbrellas
on High Street.

Misery
is tourists
looking for
`that house`
in Notting Hill.

Misery

is the queue
for the opening
of the summer sale
at Harrods.

Misery

is not much summer,
but loads of rain.

Little
Miseries

LONDON

FALL

Misery is being caught in a downpour wearing your perfectly distressed leather trainers.

Misery is trying to find a seat on the bus.

Misery

is having to fake a limp
when you realise
you've caused a queue
in front of the loo
for the disabled.

BIG BEN

Misery

is engineering work that causes a shutdown on your line.

Misery
is being served a
Marmite sandwich
for breakfast.

Misery is interrupted sleep the week of Guy Fawkes because of fireworks parties.

Misery is trying to buy a flat for under one million pounds.

Misery

is trying to get a photo of your friend in Trafalgar Square without including multiple strangers.

Misery

is trying to cross Waterloo Bridge on a windy day without being swept off your feet.

NELSONS COLUMN

Misery

is pigeon poo...
dog poo...
and fox poo
(the worst of the lot).

Misery

is forgetting to
move your car
and finding a boot
attached to the tire.

Misery

is being hit in the head
by the backpack
of the man standing
next to you on the Tube.

Misery

is everyone drunk off their arses by 7 pm on a Friday.

Misery

is walking down the street just as the pubs close.

Misery

is being an Arsenal fan.

Misery is yet another "foggy day in London town."

"When a man is tired of London, he is tired of life:
for there is in London all that life can afford."

—Samuel Johnson

Happiness

is living in one of the most diverse,
exciting cities on the planet.

...brilliant fashion, street food,
conversation, transportation.

...never being more than
5 minutes from a park.

...sharing a laugh, a chat,
cup of tea, pint of beer.

...the sun rising behind St. Paul's Cathedral.
and setting on the Thames.

LONDON is music.

LONDON is theatre.

LONDON is street life.

LONDON is nightlife.

LONDON is ancient history
and cutting-edge brand new.

London is...

HOME!